6 Mile Negus on the Honor Roll at Michigan

Justin Alexander Gordon

6 Mile Negus on the Honor Roll at Michigan

ii.

This is something for my lil smart niggas who wanna be dumb to do while they chill and blow loud at the bus stop. Reading is push-ups to the brain. I pray this strengthens you.

<u>Acknowledgements</u>

My strong foundation in the English language with its formalities started from my Pre- School teacher and grandmother, Zelma Baker. Mrs. Willie Bell Gibson was my middle school English instructor and challenged me to seek and utilize words like no other. I thank Allah, God, Yaweh, Jesus, Jesús, Issa, Yahshua and the rest for granting me the privilege of attending the best institutions inside the Detroit Public School system.

Contents

"Only a Fool would let their enemy teach their children!"

\-   Detroit Red

If My Homie Calls, Ode to Tupac Shakur

2016.
The year for forgiveness.
My homie from my hood
stole 15 and I ain't miss it.
Really, the disloyalty had me all shitty,
I'm on a new level, same day was up 60.
Made it out the hood, thought I was
representin'
But when I came back,
I was met with resentment
"You ain't really with us,
you just up and left"
Had me self-conscious, feelin' bad about
myself
Slippin back into old habits just to hang
Felt conflicted, went to the OG's for game
My barber said
"you ain't like that nigga, he a hater"
"Push forward. they on some backwards
shit, see 'em later"
Had hood dreams
take them all to the top
Wanted to stack it like Legos but they
infatuated with the block
Wanted to be legit with millions, living in
the hood

Envious niggas in my hood, ain't want me
doing good!
But its cool
Jesus loved Judas through his faults
You need help with that rent, or that bail
brody?
No problem at all,
call my phone homie.

My Network

I hang out with older niggas.
Established barbers and dope dealers.
Labor union workers
Parolees
And folk niggas.
Dreamers
Swipers
High school drop outs and broke niggas.
Cats wit GEDs,
Fast food workers and joke niggas.
Niggas wit no hope
Sell dope and who smoke niggas.
Live wit they momma
On child support
We pour 4s wit em.
Leanin
Schemin
Rap or hoop was they goals niggas.
Football pads aint fit
Then hit the road niggas.
Whole life said he wasn't shit
so heart turned cold niggas.
Fight wit the BM for his kids
That hurt his soul niggas.
Don't nobody listen
so feelins
tend to explode niggas.
Brand new prisons just built,

Come, lets grow old in em....
NO NIGGA!

They said I wouldn't make it.
They said I couldn't do it.
They said I...
Nigga shut the fuck up
You sound stupid.
Nigga you sound clueless.
No kids Imma student
On
scholarship,
not hoopin
If I drop dirty I lose it
Still smokin I'm foolin
Fuck the law, it's a nuisance
Wanna see niggas in nooses
OJ got Parole
so im juicin.

A white folks, are yall mad at that line?
I don't give a fuck, bitch
Go spazz out online
And stop lookin at my city
like we magnets to crime
Detroit vs. Everybody
Hol up
Let me tell you why..
We the blackest city
in the motha fuckin nation
so when they divide the pie
They aint tryna give us Nathan
And these fake
Detroit saviors
Really wanna see us naked
Body slam you
like Jarue
Praying to God that he make it.

<u>The time I was 18, standing at the bus stop and decided to ask a homeless man "why do people succeed and why do people fail?" after getting cliché answers about success from rich people and his response was</u>

"Cuz they want to."

NOTEtation

Hold the whole note
for four
And the half note
for two
The quaaaaaaaarter
note is simplistic and cool
The eighth note
is quick,
make turtles say "oouu"
But the 16th is fast, make
Usain Bolt
lose.

The Theory of Music, Winter 2015,
For Katri E.

It's the theory of music
If You don't use it, you lose it
You know how the summer go
People go dumb and go stupid
And semester lessons fly out
from they brain like its roofless
So here's a comprehensive lesson for you
to take to Bermuda
Or whatever beach you on
So when you bumpin' tunes up in your
speakerphone
You can visualize the science behind it
and read along.

Let's start with intervals.
Major, minor, diminished, augmented
The difference is all in the distance.
Major intervals are a half step up from
minor intervals
And augmented is larger than a major or
perfect,
It's like you climbing intervals.
Diminished is smaller and has more
specialized usage
Diminished fifth and augmented fourth
is both tri-tone music.

The circles of fifths? I ensure you its
important..
Couldn't tell you much more of it
I was insubordinate...
I was sleep like I took a punch from
George Foreman.

Now with Triads, that internal lesson can
come in handy
Put em on top of each other and the sound
can be so dandy
And really the concept is all the same
tricks
Diminished is two minors,
augmented is two majors
what you name it is where you place it!
It's a basic and comprehendible fact
You want a seventh from a triad?
just add one on top of that!

Now which sound do you want?
The Sevenths can do a lot
Do you want flats like black boys under
murderous cops?
Major, minor, dominant, augmented?
its all there for ya
Even diminished like
black people's value in America!
It's all based on which order of sharps and
flats you'd like to add
Chord progression is like writing a scale,
just make them triads!

When I was young, I was considered a
clown or a joke
I used to hang with ignorance, but I cut
down the rope.
Hope you enjoyed this lesson
I hope it touched your soul
In the words of Porky the Pig, that's all
folks!

Write-FREE in 2k8TEEN

I fight for the right, to be a kid
Battle ya for my childish fits
fight ya fa the access to my optimism...

Y we cherish freedom more while we in
prison?
Y we rushed to be grown to be when we
was young?
Y we wish to start over right when we
done?
Y do white people really wanna be black?
Y black people don't know the answer to
that?
Y they get mad at lil kids for asking
questions?
Y they say, "shhh don't challenge the
Reverend"?
Y they caution you when you tell em yo
goals?

U really know what it means to sell yo
soul?

...I fight for the right, to be ignorant.
Ignorant to the "maybes" "waits" and
"what ifs".
Battle ya for my illogical, *unreasonable*
confidence
Of this world,
I won't fight ya fa ya consciousness.

A Hip Hop Medley

The Badd and Bourgeoisie

Our system
is functioning perfect
It's not broken at all
man its working
They don't fuck with the kids that's
suburban And Detroit
is targeted on purpose

The people and cops
from the same got damn blocks
but they view
each other
as the
opps.
Realize
institution's the one that is foolin
and all this school shooting
will stop.
We hatin' each other
Not sister or brother?
Then fuck him,
don't care if he starvin'.

If we all came together, this shit would get
better
that's why they killed Malcolm and Martin.

Misogyny
Drugs
Violence
All in the music
They
influence
Got our young queens
Twerking
on the snap
Drunk
Foolin
White jews
Profit most
But the prison yard we rulin
Know the words to Migos
But
Skip Spanish class in schoolin'?

I'm the Only nigga in my classes
Rep. the city when I passed it
Show me boobies? No, that's average.
Let's get wealthy girl,
show me a math trick.

Yes, that way!
I used to call collect all day.
Yes, that way!
I seen fiends O.D in the hallway
Yes, that way!
They threw me in jail for my skin paint
Yes, that way!
The courts suck you dry for your cash
maine.

The Black's Bug

They show us rapper-athlete money
just to tease us
I done seen mo' EBTs than VISAs
Black people push the culture,
U.S need US
We pool our money together,
they'll catch a seizure

I only did three months in jail dog
Still got nightmares, what that tell y'all?
How the fuck a judge
gone' ever give a sentence
If she didn't never have to sit in it?

I did my time and came back home!
Now I'm enroooooooolled
HR see the felony
and say noooooooooooo
To get a job with a criminal record's
the hardest
It's like you're still locked up
after the bar's split.

First Day out of Fake Love

Detroit's been down so long
It looks like up to us
God, make it up to us!
The song glorifying prison just got us buzz
The irony's in our face
THE IRONY'S IN OUR FACE.

"Having soon discovered to <u>be great</u>, I must appear so, and therefore studiously avoided mixing in society, and wrapped myself in mystery, devoting my time to fasting and prayer."

-   Nat Turner

Probation Temptation, Ode to Tupac Shakur

Slow your speed down homie,
I know you see them peoples watching.
Police all up in our pocket,
I swear they all just for profit.
Niggas getting killed by cops
just from standing at the sto'.
White boy kill a church,
they put the vest on the hoe.
They ask "J,
why you always rappin' bout the struggle?
Don't you wanna just cuddle
with a woman?
that's no trouble!
I say I would
Maybe I should
You gotta understand
I caught a phony rape charge
that took away my
Backwoods.
Probation is a bitch.
Especially when you know
damn well you didn't do it
fuck it I'm grateful for my freedom
Gotta live carpe diem
Learn from past mistakes and learn how
to charm the snakes.
Living by the court's rules
up goes the stakes

Drug tests coming random
"Wanna hit?"
Naw, I'm straight.
But once in a while,
when the pressure gets to me,
Mouua Fuckas on my nerves,
I just want to roll dat doobie.
Smoke a blunt with no seeds
P.O say come in at three
Aw damn, I fell for it
Time to hit GNC
Dancing with the Devil
Plus I'm black as a kettle
Throw me in jail,
the only damn way they want to settle.
So I pray
Avoid the Temptate
So,
I can leave the state
And,
Head to LA
To get a beat from 'Ye
But so many of my homies
fell for the okedoke
Bad bitch just called, said she got some
kush to smoke...
Oh no.

Why I don't play the hunger games

my cousin asked me what was the
funniest moment I experienced in jail.
Still, bitter from the situation,
I ain't have shit to tell.
Provoked as I was to be mad at what they
aint givin
What they served every 330pm Monday
was the thing that had us trippin

peanut butter jelly for dinner
4 pieces of white bread, some cookies and
a koolaid packet

Everybody's favorite meal,
let that sink in.

These grown men of course
Commissary is kinda scary
most can't rely on support.
Sitting
Waiting
we see about six extra trays
Niggas stalkin,
hawkin,
for the best position to grab a second plate
the guard was sittin there,
a maniacal grin.

Loving his power, controlling the hunger of
men.
The guard was white,
stereotype fulfilled.
He waited til we salivated for the meal
Wanted to see us compete for it
It's just a thrill
He wait
and Say

Go! and the oppressed take off.
They would race to the tray
Pride left me hungry that day
Drank water til I felt it in my stomach that
day
wasnt no help from commissary it wasnt
comin that day

Letters was the only real food I could
consume that day.
Where would I be if i would have
Mandingo fought over food that day.

#ForTheAmericanCulture

Education and incarceration
I did it simultaneous
Repeated nightmares of doing homework
when I was caged in
Until your freedom is taken
You don't have true veneration
About doing your homework
About writing that paper
That you procrastinate on
Saying "I'll do it later."
How would you feel if your lights went off
when the guard say?
Supplies taken away,
Books coming?
Not today
Ink pens are not accepted
Considered a weapon
Then you left with
A half pencil with a little lead
So you regret you must protect it
And pray that the nigga you bunk with
don't try and get it.

The jail packed tight
Just to write
You might
not have no room
And not to mention the stress that is
courtrooms

Before the jailhouse
After the bailout
Counting down the days
Fear of takin' that cell route

I had a 3.9
before I got locked up for the third time
Stressing in and out of court that
semester got me a 3.0
Average the cumulative That's a 3.4
Black man's mistakes plus the systems a
snake
That's what it'll get you
On the paddy wagon saying "Look what I
got into."

God blessed me with options I could sit,
or get it poppin
The mail came
Opened my homework up

Let's get to rockin'
Blocked out the screams
Held on to my dreams
Didn't drop 'em.

And when they said I couldn't take my
paperwork with me
That didn't stop him!
Jail or on trial, Ben Wallace couldn't even
block him
I can't rest til the rest of my niggas
got the same options.

Zay

2023 just seems so far away
For my nigga sake I'm goin hard today
We got the same charge
but way different case
Fuck the system, wanna see a nigga break
I aint never scared, I won't never shake
On the way to get this money
I aint runnin late.

Remember sitting on Archdale, kush had
us baked.

Remember L, the weedman? You ain't like
that nigga, talked about robbin that nigga.
I'm glad you didn't. It was funny to hear
you talk shit about him all the way til we
bought the weed and smoked his product
happily.

I just remembered I can't talk about
crimes and send this to you. Damn.
That would be like dry snitchin on you
and myself. Phew. I'm glad
I remembered before I threw
This in the mail.

That was God's plan to jail me next to you
I knew when i returned home I would ball
for two

Couldn't trust a dumb criminal locked up
who got caught, most them was lames.
So I stayed to myself, me and you,
playin pushup games
Face eachother, do a push up,
then slap hands to count one
Saving cookies and kool aid packets
To share on our bunks, shit stunk.
But we had eachother... for a min.
I was goin home, you was goin to prison
I did three months, you 8 year biddin,
you younger than me.
Damn this system vicious

You aint really have no pops growin up,
did ya?
You was out there on yo own,
you had to get it.
Nigga ran up on you talkin crazy,
had to stick em
It was gone be yo life or his,
and you was on a mission
And you aint even kill em,
damn you shoulda killt em.
So he couldn't run his fuckin mouth,
which caused the sentence.
No face, no case, nigga,
you know the business
You put him on a shit bag,
but Im mad he out here livin.
You blew a chunk out of his ass,
im mad he still kickin.

My bad, you caught me in a moment,
Jesus please forgive me.

But that nigga played gangsta, til them
bullets hit em
Coulda said he aint see you,
but he chose the side of the system.
Now he the police, you badge ass nigga
Helped them take my nigga 20s
You a stuck in the bucket, Mr. Krabs ass
nigga.

Back to you Zay,
I cant live in the past tense
I pray you forgive that man, since,
Forgiveness is self love, but
He ain't want you alive!
He was ready to take yo life, you was
justified!
I read yo letters and know you'll survive
You will never be forgotten thru yo nigga's
rhymes.

When we was young, 15-16,
You was standing on yo porch, drunk,
pissy
You said "what yall bitches up to" to me
and my cousin
At the time I brushed that shit off,
like it was nothing.
But that shit hurt me, I know you was
drunk, you prolly aint mean nth by it,

But that shit stung.
Words hurt, but we men now
We gotta make the sacrifices, save our kin
now.

I don't know, my nigga, just wanted to
write to you. But its fucked up I can't send
this kite to you.
To much truth up in this poem,
ion want get us in trouble
And you know guidelines say we aint
sposed to be talkin to eachother.
Fuck it, imma just give it to the world,
clears my throat
Maybe they can appreciate the art, you
know how life go.
Take a nigga pain, make something
beautiful.
Imma get rich off this shit.
So you can never again have to have dope
residue all in yo cuticles.

If you hear the dogs, keep going. If you see the torches in the woods, keep going. If there's shouting after you, keep going. Don't ever stop. Keep going. If you want a taste of freedom, keep going.

- Harriet Tubman

Hold your Head, Ode to Tupac Shakur

Perhaps I should shut up and take it
I know how to make the money
It's so easy to fake it.
fuck it lets face it.
We rather say "free my niggas"
And wear shirts with dead faces
Let's stop being so brainless.

Instead, be proactive with the route that
we takin
Only cowards judge a man if they ain't
helpin' him make it
Won't even dig in yo pockets
sacrifice Ten dollars
But when the judge give him that time
you get to hoopin and hollerin'
Oh Lord, we weak!
It's gotta be another way
Niggas cry that broke shit,
but then smoke everyday.

"Oh you got a new whip and chain,
I bet I do better"
It never cross they mind to
come together for cheddar
Will this way of thinking ever stop?
Probably never.

I pray Willie Lynch burns in hell with a
Cosby Sweater.

I still got hope
for the real and the true
I wish y'all could see
that trap shit they talking
outside of the booth. (Hmm.)
But while they steady glorifying all that
Paaaaaiiiinnnnnn.
It's the same motha fuckas
that left the hood
and neva came back
once that check came.

Damn Harriet!

Think I'm playin?
You wanna go back? The fuck you mean
you wanna go back?
Nigga I asked you before we left
was you sure you wanna do this.
You coulda stayed.
You coulda slaved some more.
You was mister big dick then. Hmm?
Wanted to show everybody you wasn't
scared.
That you was tired of getting yo ass
whupped for no reason.
Master fucked lil Dorothea and I know you
still hurt by that. That was yo woman.
You said you wasn't standing for that
no more.
Master gave you 10 lashings when he
caught you with that book. You said you
ain't standing for that.
Yo child got sold down to the Johnson
plantation bout three months after she
was born.
I remember you tellin me that.
You lookin to follow this North star is what
you told me. But now you bitchin up.
Alright, alright. I feel you. I understand
you don't wanna leave yo family behind.

You wished big momma came witcha.
I feel that.
It was tough leaving your girl, it would
have been too risky for her to leave from
under the surveillance of the master.
You was just about to get promoted to stay
in the house too!
Right, right. You swear not to tell on us in
the event that you get caught going back.
Look,
I know you responsible enough not to put
us and the whole underground railroad in
jeopardy. I trust you fam!
Go head, no hard feelings. That star there
will lead you back to the plantation.
Bye Percy!
(Pow.)
Now who the fuck else wanna go back?

Kick Ass

"(I'm) scary like black people with ideas."
- Kanye West

I kick ass when I hopped on campus,
fresh out tha cuffs.
I kick ass when I make niggas boss up
without the buffs.
I kick ass when I say
just makin it aint enough,
I kick ass when I hear God's voice
sayin "nut up!"

Muhammad Ali kicked ass.
I aint talkin in the ring.
Walked it like he talked it,
into existence spoke his dreams.
Floatin like a butterfly
Stangin like a bee
When he didn't go to Vietnam,
he was crowned King.
They Drafted him, Harassing him
"Oh we gone shut that
loud
ass
mouth
now"
Laughed at him.

Getting ya ass kicked,
kinda sounds like this:
"You gotta compromise your beliefs,
or we won't let you compete."

See, Ali,
at the time,
was Boxing's world champ.
But he was drug free, outspoken, and had
God in his camp.
Impenetrable character
To the devil? nothing scarier.
He would pull up to the hood to inspire
the youth in the area!

He stood up to that white man
would NOT fight in they war
Banned him for three years from boxing
And he is the GOAT for it.

I kick ass when the spirit of legends
live on through me.
I kick ass when I sacrifice
my life for the movement.
I kick ass when I acknowledge
a mistake I make,
I kick ass when I ain't never scared
to say I'm great.

Protest with Paper

If you still shop at H&M,
we can't be friends.
Boycott bullshit.
Strike a snake.
Give no money to those misers.
Miserly to the people yet generous when
they need you.
MLK started telling people to
protest with paper.
He died shortly after. Duh!
That's how you know it's working.
Give your life up for someone else's license
to live.
If your protest is orderly in the eyes of
pigs, that ain't no damn protest.
Money motivates these modern-day
morons who act as Monarchs
over me And you.
So why not hit the pockets?
This economy is driven by consumption,
so why can't we organize what we
consume?
Let's not support ALL of the companies
who benefit from inhumane prison labor,
right?
There may be too many to actually boycott
them all at once, but dammit I'll start with
one.

McDonald's, Starbucks, shit, Jordan, the
list goes on and on.
You probably thinking,
"what does a poet know?
Your claim to fame is to make the words
do the action, while the leg work is what's
needed."
The ink of a scholar is worth more than
the blood of a martyr
Heed my words- let's go farther.
And if the time comes to take my track
shoes out and run with you...
What am I saying, that time was
yesterday.
That time was last year.
So, when I'm in the streets and I may need
to spend my money.
I take out my cash and ask,
would Matulu approve this purchase?

"Every time there's a revolution, it comes from somebody reading a book about revolution. David Walker wrote a book and Nat Turner did his thing."

- Mike Tyson

Death Around the Corner, Ode to Tupac Shakur

Friday night grind
Make it feel like a Monday
Work Sunday
Forgive my niggas for they gunplay
We don't know no better!
In this rat race chasin' cheddar
Rock hoodies together
RIP Trayvon Martin FOREVER
But if a nigga step on my toes
Imma explode
Don't get touched on,
tryna show off for hoes
My heart is cold
It's bad because I wear it on my sleeve
I'm from Detroit,
where the high is 20 degrees.
So if it falls off and breaks,
I'll be more than relieved.
Therefore it's no emotion
Just focus,
murder and leave.
I need a reprieve.
My P.O tryna violate my probation
Trying to stop my education
Wants to see me out here naked
Got opportunities to explore the world
I'm denied because I'm a felon
Man I ain't rape that fuckin' girl!

17 in a mad man's dream
Using jail phones to make my girl's
"Hotline Bling"
but I ain't innocent. damn sure had that
weed on me.
And when they tested me. damn sure
wasn't clean homie.
The War on Drugs is really the War on
Niggas
Prisons filled, so no wonder why the
school kids missin'.

Maybe Next Lifetime

Ok, any guy that can confidently wear an
orange hat that isn't homeless
must have something Extra to him.
Fuck, his stare is gentle enough for me to
reciprocate
Yet intense enough to turn me on.
Corny jokes feed me,
through my blush he can read me;
I'm enjoying this familiar moment with
this.. Stranger.
I wonder, is his cock big?
I wonder does he lick pussy correctly.
He is so attracted to me, he can't even
play it cool.
I kinda like that.
He's too much of a straight shooter.
If I didn't have a boyfriend,
I'd turn his page with no bookmark,
Spill ink all over him and watch him read
my notes,
Maybe a number for him to call...
But, I'm loyal to my man,
So these words never will publish,
At all.

Adventures with Harriet
"Downdrotten peoples"

"God is the most misunderstood."
                                        -Rakeem

I ain't walk my ass up and down this
country For nothin!
When we get to the north, nigga,
you betta get to hustlin.
Be somethin.
Think of all yo peoples
that's still strugglin.
You see what happened to Percy!?
Don't make me get to bussin!

I'm only rollin wit soldiers.
That "woe is me" shit's over.
'Got the world on dese, B
Can't cry on my shoulder.

God gave me them orders straight.

Niggas go through hell just to
get enough money to look heaven sent
Negligent.
Sellin yo sole
is going under yo potential.
for a watch,
chain
or an assault
with a pistol.
Slave mentality casualties like
crabs in a bucket
We beefin cuz we tough
but even more
didn't get love enough.

School is boring
That shit is worse
That shit is horrid.
Black kids fight
shots by whites
both just human being mistreatment.
Eurocentric methods are uprooting
themselves
the system aint broken
its workin quite well.

Capitalism must have a winner and a
loser.
They gave us the bible
took the land
they make up all the rules
we got the preacher stand.

The World continues to roll..
As cyclical natures go..
Browns and blacks get back
To power
Am I ready for that role?
Is my patience in tune with the respect for
each human sole?
Can I treat the rich man the same way I
treat the po'?
Can we love white people and forgive them
even though
They fucked us when we put em on,
then acted like some hoes?

I'm Tired

I'm so tired of my niggas goin thru shit
I'm so tired of the options as rappin,
slangin or hoopin
Well I'm rappin
But trust me I'm rappin
to give my two cent
Well fuck two cent,
I want money like im hoopin
But First priority is to inspire change
Goin platinum aint gone do shit
Guys just have envious eyes and
feel like they losin'
So my niggas here lies my word,
If you love me, hold me to it.
When I get rich, Imma live like Jesus and
don't abuse it
Pay off my people's debts,
Be in the hood but not to flex
But to be proximate, touchable so we
never forget
I wont forget where I came from,
you wont forget we can go farther
I aint runnin to live with white folks, I'll be
right here tomorrow.

Cuz Im tired man.

Im tired

Im tired Im tired

Man Im tired man. Im tired

Im tired Im tired

Man Im tired man, IM TIRED

IM TIRED

 IM TIRED

MAN IM TIRED!

(And I aint being quiet.)

I'm tired of niggas reading off paper.
I'm tired of seeing niggas love paper.
I'm tired of seeing niggas on papers.

I'm so tired of niggas talkin bout Lakers.
Except. Lavar Ball. He's the best. We need
that. I digress.
Now I love sports, so take time to listen.
If these athletes cared about the cause,
They wouldn't let they boss call them
"inmates that's running the prison!"
Is you kiddin?
Most these niggas came from the hood,
poverty
Now y'all millionaires, and y'all sayin
y'all can't shut all that shit down?
Don't lie to me.

Now If just half of the black stars in the
NFL
Said we aint playin a game til 50 thousand
make bail
Or if Lebron and some other stars in the
NBA
Said we gone play at Rucker
til Kapernick gets to play.

You think it won't happen?
You think them white folks gone have it?

51

You think they gone let all that money fall
away...
What about madden?
What about 2k?
If athletes who had a fuckin backbone was
to say "You cant put our likeness on those
games
Not to-day!
Until we get some better schools
Criminal Justice System get better rules
We ain't putting on jerseys for you racist
ass fools!"

Cuz Im tired of the evil
And this just one of my solutions
Dis my PSA for ballplayers
Let's see if they gone do it.

Im tired.

Hustle in my Blood

10 hour
days
for the shift then I am
yo slave.
Dreams awakened
Yo irrigation's my wave.

You can climb on top or be under me
You hunger me
To provide a life
with a wife
Who comforts me.

Delicate gentleness,
Passionate, silly shit,
Laughin and gigglin,
Best friend I kick it wit.

Khadijah and Muhammad
The one that I get
that chicken wit.
God sends down
his blessings
and you the one that
I split it wit.
Roll weed, get close to
Jesus and you the one
that I hit it wit.

Gavel bang that time,
You the one I do that
sentence wit Cuz

Hustle in my blood
Day or night it don't matter
We get it out the mud.
I pray to God for the strength
to be someone you can trust .
I put that ring on yo finger
fuckin you not enough.
I want yo love.

Menaje Trais
Me you
and our God
We run shit
in Détroit
All the way
to Algeria,
We love on earth
we holdin hands. We argue
then we love again
And if we become
mother man
We show our kids
the motherland.

Our royalty is deep
Your loyalty's most sexy
that's a promise I can keep
I wanna meet yo needs

And rub softly on them knees
as they buckle
My dick get hard
because I see you get weak
When I touch you.
Super bad, just one
of the reasons I love you.
The three sexiest words you ever said was
"I trust you."

Make love to my mentor Someone I can
look
up to
And it's yo choice baby,
You can leave when you want to
Or you can,
Breathe on me
Cream on me
Period, Bleed on me
Joe Clark
Lean on me.

If I'm off, keep on me.
Cuz, It's hustle in this blood.

"Let us pick up our books and pencils. They are our most powerful weapon."

- Malala Yousafzai

Lord Knows, Ode to Tupac Shakur

I wanna support my girl and give her
the world
right now its about gas in the whip,
Its no bread for the pearls.
Drink that Henny 'til I earl
after the dumbbells I curl
Cuz the liquor numb me up and niggas
know that I'm thorough
Not quick to fight,
but will defend my life.
I'm suicidal, so keep that Glock
Up out of my sight
Because I might
just
use it on myself, or a cop
who abuse my rights
If it's Corrections, why do they give people
life?
They don't want you to improve your
mistakes
Blacks were here first, so niggas,
know yo place
That's all bullshit, about that "Aryan" race
Stop calling whites Caucasian because
that shit is so fake
Check it.

The word comes from people from the
Caucasus mountains
Who thought they were better than YOU
Yeah, I researched and I found it.
They thought they were the pure ones
fresh up out the dirt
But that's wrong
So when you say it, It's yourself you hurt.
This self- hatred shit, has gone way too far
You want to see who's real or fake? See
how they act in the dark.
Niggas get killed in the streets,
and then we march
But protesting and riots only go so far.
It's eye for an eye, fight fire with fire.
Come together with our paper,
watch America perspire.

Adventures with Harriet
"Enlightening is Frightening"

"When you got niggas working you can't
show em everything. Cuz niggas get to
feelin like you owe em everything."
-Doughboy Scooch

Tell a lost nigga too much truth
It's overwhelming.
To let you know all my routes
It's kinda scary.
What if they really an informant?
Let them thoughts lay dormant, rest yo
eyes around a snake and it's a wrap
By the morning.

A hatin ass nigga aint born, it's a process
when they cross you.
Resentment, jealousy, by- any -means
ambition, greed,
All precede the action.
Staying out the way of that,
requires moving with tact.

Freeing niggas is against the law
And when you breaking the law
Evaluate carefully who you callin yo dogs.
Too many cooks in the kitchen
Is pollution to your mission

TOO MANY CHIEFS, NOT ENOUGH
INDIANS.
Revolutions go missin, just a word from
experience.

When you show someone the truth,
tell them in portions at a time,
too much is overwhelming
4 they health
And if you the boss, go wit yo gut feeling
when it tell you-
keep some shit to yourself.

My Movie on Malcolm X ain't done yet

"You can ask everybody for their opinion,
but the last decision has to be yours."
- Unc Dex

The bible suggests seeking wise counsel
when making decisions.
A pigeon cannot understand an Eagle's
position.
I caution less that your words may fall on
deaf ears,
but more so the response that you seek
May come from a perspective of fear.
"You should do this!"
"You should do that!"
"No, do that!"
"But what about this!"
"Your chances are like a needle in a
haystack."
"No, that doesn't make sense!"

"It's only a one in a million chance!"
"You aint gon make no money like that!
You just don't understand!"

Energies like these
will have the strongest on their knees
And you'll look up
Huff and puff
Cuz you workin towards
someone else's dream.

They'll call you wild, when you really just
out the box
They'll say you rushin it, like they
mastered the clock
You ready to take flight,
they'll caution you on everything that
ain't right.
Only cuz back in the day,
when they scraped their knee,
they got scared of the bike.

People project their fears unto
your ambition
Cuz you got the balls to
do something they didn't.

So my Malcolm X movie ain't finished,
not cuz I don't have the vision
But everybody had an opinion
I let too many cooks up in the kitchen.

Be different.
If you a eagle, be a eagle, and watch out
for them pigeons.
Cuz they'll say "that's impossible!"
---- Until you did it.

Ten commandments to stay out of jail

this rap is 4 survival reasons.
Introduced to this world since my teens
17 years old
police knocked on momma's door
Evading a cell while trapped on felony
probation,
all throughout my adult ages
State of Michigan's what I'm caged in
Been arrested four times
The objective of this rhyme
Is 4 you to save some money and not give
them bitches yo time

1.

Nombre Uno
Keep paperwork to a minimum
cash Is priority
No paper trail even on the lapel of your
favorite sweater
Take the cash off the card at the ATM
soon as you get it
Tickets and all that shit,
pay ASAP
Keep yo name off lists and all statements
Especially to those stATE men
You got it?
OK then.

2.

number two
play like chess, stay ahead two moves.
Always keep a legit hustle
even if its part time
it helps legitimize your struggle
and its a great cover if you is doin dirt
You gotta alibi
at a company,
wit a clerk.

3.

No co defendant
means
better hope when defendin.
You know not to do no dirt wit that man.
You know Kimberly Elise
aint down for that plan.
Nobody wants to be that tough, doing their
friend's time.
I can bro you all day but really only got
one brother.
So Bro, when you the smartest person in
the room, go and find another.

NUMBER 4.

I know you heard this before...
"I refuse to speak. You, officer, shall hear
from my attorney."

5.

Don't be tryna fuck the women of jealous
niggas. That shit will turn into a case
quicker than the ending.
"When bitches get horny, niggas die."
Tupac told us.
A jealous man will throw his life away for
that bonin
that took you two weeks' worth of game
and ten min of strokin.

McNichols!

What's rollin in the car u n?
What you got up on yo person?
If she already got priors
The space just might get raided
Police inherently crooked
That's Just they history
Put us monkeys in the cage
When we criticized the tree.
Understand the company
You keep, is in your hands.
If he holdin and he don't tell you,
and you got a record, he is not yo mans.

Seven.

That school route is a cool route
Judge hear that shit and automatically
give clout
It aint for everybody, i know. Hell, it
wasn't even built for us!
But if yo hustle aint in sumthen, you cant
do shit for us.
<u>Take advantage of poverty, knock that</u>
<u>paperwork out properly</u>
<u>Get them schollies and grants</u>
<u>leave them,</u>
<u>Loans alone.</u>
That white man education can pay on its
own
If not that, than a skill, trade, just a
certification in something that required
patience.

8.

Learn to read more and save more money
Reading don't make you a ham
Not reading makes you a dummy
u continuously got the ups on information
wit the readin skill
Put away way more than you spend so
when the lawyer get it right the first time
NO need 4 appeals

Number 9 shoulda been number 1 to me.

Don't think jail a badge of honor that real niggas gotta complete.
The state pen got the pinned's state of mind with a feeling of capture and isolation.
We must not just avoid that, but destroy.

the last stand of slavery in amerikkka is in the Prison Industrial Complex,
breaking generational curses by not absorbing negative thoughts about yourself.
rappers sure do talk a lot about the shit that gets us cooked. You peeped that?

And number ten.

A strong word called humility.
Keeps you out of they reach.
and people on yo team.

and even if she coming down with a
sentence
she might ban you
but 10 beat 20.

Follow these rules..
probation you still facin.
this shit aint perfect
its target marks up on our jerseys
They playing wit 30s
Steph Curry
Our kids hurting
They gettin hit
From Grade 3 they marked 4it.

Or you can be clean,
go to Howard/Harvard start on they team
pop star at 19
leave the country right when you please
smoke weed whenever you want!

I gotta skate
because MDOC don't like what I say,
these the ten stay out of jail
commandments,
Free the apes.

When I lived Today

Arrogant asswipes is always demanding tissue
Bitch ass COs stuck in jail, too, tryna get you
Cds floppin cuz niggas aint respect the pencil
Double Ds distracting dumbasses that trick in rentals
Easy E died cuz of a quest for chasing pussy
Fuck The Terminator, he aint shit for killin Tookie
Gangsta wannabes is just practice for Cop rookies
Hell I wanted to visit, asked a crack head, so he took me.
Intellectuals tend to lose faith and trust what's certain
Justin follow dat boy born straight from the virgin
Kill the noise, Trump did make America great
Losing Clinton helps us unveil bullshit and face the hate
Most of the country mad at me, cuz i'm takin a knee
Not considering the plea for my safety
Oh say can you see? Francis Scott Key
Proud that black folks still in slavery
Questions about the Vatican get covered up
Restless minds wanna know how they murdered us
Serious thinkers know black history is hidden
Too many cover ups with sports and drug dealin
U've all seen how blacks refuse to settle down
Victors write the history but listen to these sounds
Winning isnt always in the money
Xanax is a legal drug dealer, fuck they company
Y schools closing, prisons opening in this country?
Zenith capitalism preys on the poor and hungry.

Cuz Actors sposed to Act, and Rappers sposed to rap

What if I told you the NFL wasn't for
blacks?
What if I told you we got law degrees
instead of that?
What if I told you, really,
you can have it all?
Would you say "I don't have the time" and
just laugh me off?
What if I told you, you can be an
actor, lawyer, singer,
activist, author, and an all- American
football teamer?
What if I told you thinking small is for the
past?
And everything you do would be world
class?
Would you say "got damn, that's too many
choices"
What if I told you, "no, don't listen to them
voices!"

What if I told you his name was Paul
Robeson?

Oh, that's right, the school books ain't
show you him.
Revolutionize yo mind,
don't take my word for it
go read his book for yourself, called
Here I Stand
Don't depend on me or no one else
to give you knowledge
Cuz in the end
You play
Wit yo own hand
So read it
Audio book the shit if needed
And learn how the government
black balled him
For speaking
On issues
using his platform like some tissue
Clearing the bullshit
out our path
so we can get to
The facts.
And yall know they hate that
 Cuz actors sposed to act
And rappers sposed to rap
Right?
And if you agree, goodnight
I'm not talking to you Guys,
Get out my sight
Robeson used his privilege so right
Fought against plight
For poor people black and white

Racism. Kapernick aint the first nigga they hated
Hollywood told him "yo days is numbered, keep playin"
Wit house money
Paul told em "im no dummy"
Uncle Tom or a Flunkie,
Sellout or a Junkie.
See he was getting money
A list star
Name up in lights,
Had a
A list broad
As his wife Family, kids
He set for life.
But instead of keeping silent, He chose to use his light.

Goodnight.

Instagram: @detroitgordon
Facebook: Justin Gordon (Detroit)
But the best way is to catch me in traffic.
The revolution still will not be televised, or
tweeted.

Jordyn Fishman is a student at the Penny Stamps School of Art and Design at the University of Michigan. Her artwork is focused on celebrating love. Fishman has shown her work in various exhibitions including the Grand Rapids Art Museum for ArtPrize Nine.
Website: jordynfishman.com
instagram: @jordyn_fishman

Made in the USA
Monee, IL
07 July 2020